Midwest

AMERICAN REGIONAL COOKING LIBRARY
Culture, Tradition, and History

African American

American Indian

Amish and Mennonite

California

Hawaiian

Louisiana

Mexican American

Mid–Atlantic

Midwest

New England

Northwest

Southern

Southern Appalachia

Texas

Thanksgiving

Midwest

Mason Crest Publishers
Philadelphia

Mason Crest Publishers Inc.
370 Reed Road
Broomall, Pennsylvania 19008
(866) MCP-BOOK (toll free)
www.masoncrest.com

First printing
1 2 3 4 5 6 7 8 9 10

Library of Congress Cataloging-in-Publication Data

Libal, Joyce.
   Midwest / compiled by Joyce Libal.
      p. cm. — (American regional cooking library)
   Includes index.
   ISBN 1-59084-616-8
   1. Cookery, American—Midwestern style—Juvenile literature. I. Title. II. Series.
   TX715.2.M53L53 2005
   741.5977—dc22
                                         2004007580
Compiled by Joyce Libal.
Recipes by Patricia Therrien.
Recipes tested and prepared by Bonni Phelps.
Produced by Harding House Publishing Services, Inc., Vestal, New York.
Interior design by Dianne Hodack.
Cover design by Michelle Bouch.
Printed and bound in the Hashemite Kingdom of Jordan.

Contents

Introduction
by the Culinary Institute of America

Cooking is a dynamic profession, one that presents some of the greatest challenges and offers some of the greatest rewards. Since 1946, the Culinary Institute of America has provided aspiring and seasoned foodservice professionals with the knowledge and skills needed to become leaders and innovators in this industry.

Here at the CIA, we teach our students the fundamental culinary techniques they need to build a sound foundation for their foodservice careers. There is always another level of perfection for them to achieve and another skill to master. Our rigorous curriculum provides them with a springboard to continued growth and success.

Food is far more than simply sustenance or the source of energy to fuel you and your family through life's daily regimen. It conjures memories throughout life, summoning up the smell, taste, and flavor of simpler times. Cooking is more than an art and a science; it provides family history. Food prepared with care epitomizes the love, devotion, and culinary delights that you offer to your friends and family.

A cuisine provides a way to express and establish customs—the way a food should taste and the flavors and aromas associated with that food. Cuisines are more than just a collection of ingredients, cooking utensils, and dishes from a geographic location; they are elements that are critical to establishing a culinary identity.

When you can accurately read a recipe, you can trace a variety of influences by observing which ingredients are selected and also by noting the technique that is used. If you research the historical origins of a recipe, you may find ingredients that traveled from East to West or from the New World to the Old. Traditional methods of cooking a dish may have changed with the times or to meet the special challenges.

The history of cooking illustrates the significance of innovation and the trading or sharing of ingredients and tools between societies. Although the various cooking vessels over the years have changed, the basic cooking methods have remained the same. Through adaptation, a recipe created years ago in a remote corner of the world could today be recognized by many throughout the globe.

When observing the customs of different societies, it becomes apparent that food brings people together. It is the common thread that we share and that we value. Regardless of the occasion, food is present to celebrate and to comfort. Through food we can experience other cultures and lands, learning the significance of particular ingredients and cooking techniques.

As you begin your journey through the culinary arts, keep in mind the power that food and cuisine holds. When passed from generation to generation, family heritage and traditions remain strong. Become familiar with the dishes your family has enjoyed through the years and play a role in keeping them alive. Don't be afraid to embellish recipes along the way – creativity is what cooking is all about.

Midwest Culture, History, and Traditions

From the far north where Laura Ingalls Wilder wrote Little House in the Big Woods, south to the state of Kansas (where families were so embroiled in the morality issues of the Civil War that the state became known as "Bloody Kansas"), lies the Midwest. Its east to west boundaries are just as impressive. "America's breadbasket" stretches from the Ohio/Pennsylvania border in the east, across the great prairie, almost to the Rocky Mountains. A dozen states (Ohio, Michigan, Indiana, Wisconsin, Illinois, Minnesota, Iowa, Missouri, North Dakota, South Dakota, Nebraska, and Kansas), containing some of the most fertile soils in America, compose the vast area known as "the Midwest."

Countless American Indian tribes had already been making use of the area's bounty for centuries. Eventually, the Indians were forced onto reservations, some locally and others to "Indian territory" that was established in Kansas, but their original presence is still recognized today in the many Indian names for these states, their geographic features, and their cities.

In the 1800s, the rich soils of the Midwest enticed immigrants from many countries, including Germany, Norway, and Sweden. When these hardy folks settled the country's interior in the nineteenth and early twentieth centuries, they brought their farming and cooking traditions with them. Areas closest to water for transportation to market were prime locations for settlement. Cereal grains such as corn and oats were grown, but the most important crop was wheat. Today, Chicago, the third largest city in the United States and an important shipping port on Lake Michigan, is a transportation center. Here rail and air transport systems also meet, allowing shipment of agricultural goods across the country.

Ohio and Wisconsin were among the major areas for German settlement, but smaller groups also formed communities. In the Keweenaw Peninsula of Michigan, you'll find descendants of Cornish miners from England along with Finns and Swedes. In Kansas, you'll find descendants of the two hundred African American settlers who

established a settlement in the 1870s. Between 1850 and 1870 immigrants from Denmark took up residence in every county in that state. Kansas became home to many people from Croatia in the 1880s. There are also many Mennonites of German-Russian origin and a great many Hispanic people.

Immigration continues even in the twenty-first century, and today you can find communities with many people from Cambodia as well as other Asian countries. The Midwest is a true crossroads of cultures.

Despite this incredibly diverse background, some foods are thought of as traditionally Midwestern. Generally, they can be described as simple comfort foods. Midwest cooking is creative, but the taste is uncluttered; you won't find a high degree of spicy ingredients. In addition to cereal grains, summer fields are lush with foods like snap beans, peas, sweet corn, and strawberries. Wisconsin leads the nation in the production of cranberries, and Illinois is the top producer of pumpkins and horseradish. All these foods find their way to the farm table, but Midwest winters are harsh. Pioneer families needed to preserve food to carry them through many months. Pickling vegetables, including green beans and beets, was one method used, and it's still a popular method of food preservation among some families. Root vegetables last for many months if kept under the ground. Their popularity continues today as does that of cured meats and sausages. Fish from the many lakes of the Upper Midwest provided food year round, as did livestock kept on family farms. The Midwest houses one of the most important dairy areas of America. Rich cheese and lush desserts are also part of Midwest food culture.

This book invites you to savor some of the food traditions that have become hallmarks of "America's heartland," the Midwest.

Before you cook...

If you haven't done much cooking before, you may find recipe books a little confusing. Certain words and terms can seem unfamiliar. You may find the measurements difficult to understand. What appears to be an easy or familiar dish may contain ingredients you've never heard of before. You might not understand what utensil the recipe calls for you to use, or you might not be sure what the recipe is asking you to do.

Reading the pages in this section before you get started may help you understand the directions better so that your cooking goes more smoothly. You can also refer back to these pages whenever you run into questions.

Safety Tips

Cooking involves handling very hot and very sharp objects, so being careful is common sense. What's more, you want to be certain that anything you plan on putting in your mouth is safe to eat. If you follow these easy tips, you should find that cooking

Minneapolis, Minnesota

Before you cook...

- Always wash your hands before and after handling food. This is particularly important after you handle raw meats, poultry, and eggs, as bacteria called salmonella can live on these uncooked foods. You can't see or smell salmonella, but these germs can make you or anyone who swallows them very sick.
- Make a habit of using potholders or oven mitts whenever you handle pots and pans from the oven or microwave.
- Always set pots, pans, and knives with their handles away from counter edges. This way you won't risk catching your sleeves on them—and any younger children in the house won't be in danger of grabbing something hot or sharp.
- Don't leave perishable food sitting out of the refrigerator for more than an hour or two.
- Wash all raw fruits and vegetables to remove dirt and chemicals.
- Use a cutting board when chopping vegetables or fruit, and always cut away from yourself.
- Don't overheat grease or oil—but if grease or oil does catch fire, don't try to extinguish the flames with water. Instead, throw baking soda or salt on the fire to put it out. Turn all stove burners off.
- If you burn yourself, immediately put the burn under cold water, as this will prevent the burn from becoming more painful.
- Never put metal dishes or utensils in the microwave. Use only microwave-proof dishes.
- Wash cutting boards and knives thoroughly after cutting meat, fish or poultry — especially when raw and before using the same tools to prepare other foods such as vegetables and cheese. This will prevent the spread of bacteria such as salmonella.
- Keep your hands away from any moving parts of appliances, such as mixers.
- Unplug any appliance, such as a mixer, blender, or food processor before assembling for use or disassembling after use.

Metric Conversion Table

Most cooks in the United States use measuring containers based on an eight-ounce cup, a teaspoon, and a tablespoon. Meanwhile, cooks in Canada and Europe are more apt to use metric measurements. The recipes in this book use cups, teaspoons, and tablespoons—but you can convert these measurements to metric by using the table below.

Temperature
To convert Fahrenheit degrees to Celsius, subtract 32 and multiply by .56.

212°F = 100°C
(this is the boiling point of water)
250°F = 110°C
275°F = 135°C
300°F = 150°C
325°F = 160°C
350°F = 180°C
375°F = 190°C
400°F = 200°C

Liquid Measurements
1 teaspoon = 5 milliliters
1 tablespoon = 15 milliliters
1 fluid ounce = 30 milliliters
1 cup = 240 milliliters
1 pint = 480 milliliters
1 quart = 0.95 liters
1 gallon = 3.8 liters

Measurements of Mass or Weight
1 ounce = 28 grams
8 ounces = 227 grams
1 pound (16 ounces) = 0.45 kilograms
2.2 pounds = 1 kilogram

Measurements of Length
¼ inch = 0.6 centimeters
½ inch = 1.25 centimeters
1 inch = 2.5 centimeters

Pan Sizes

Baking pans are usually made in standard sizes. The pans used in the United States are roughly equivalent to the following metric pans:

9-inch cake pan = 23-centimeter pan
11x7-inch baking pan = 28x18-centimeter baking pan
13x9-inch baking pan = 32.5x23-centimeter baking pan
9x5-inch loaf pan = 23x13-centimeter loaf pan
2-quart casserole = 2-liter casserole

Useful Tools, Utensils, Dishes

candy thermometer

cast-iron skillet

cheese shredder

Dutch oven

electric mixer

flour sifter

garlic press

jelly roll pan

pancake griddle   ring mold   stockpot

turkey baster   wire whisk   mallet

Cooking Glossary

cream   A term used to describe mixing sugar with butter or shortening until they are light and well blended.

cut   Mix solid shortening or butter into flour, usually by using a pastry blender or two knives and making short, chopping strokes until the mixture looks like small pellets.

dash   A very small amount, just a couple of drops.

diced   Cut into small cubes or pieces.

dollop   A small mound, about 1 or 2 tablespoons.

dredge To coat meat or seafood with flour or crumbs usually by dragging or tossing.

fillets Thin strips of boneless fish or meat.

hulled A seed that has had the hard, outer covering removed.

knead To work dough with the hands, lifting the far edge, placing it upon the rest, and pushing with the heal of the hands.

mince Cut into very small pieces.

puree A paste or thick liquid suspension usually made from finely ground cooked food.

sauté Fry in a skillet over high heat while stirring.

set When a food preparation has completed the thickening process and can be sliced.

simmer Gently boiling, so that the surface of the liquid just ripples gently.

slivered Cut very thin.

smorgasbord A lunch or dinner buffet offering many different foods.

stock Liquid used as a basis for gravy, soup, or sauce in which meat, fish, or seafood has been simmered.

whisk Stir briskly with a wire whisk.

Special Midwest Flavors

garlic

honey

maple syrup

mustard

vinegar

Midwest Recipes

Buckwheat Pancakes

Buckwheat pancakes have been popular among folks on the prairie since the 1800s.

Preheat pancake griddle.

Ingredients:

½ cup buckwheat flour

1½ cups flour

½ teaspoon salt

1 teaspoon baking soda

2 eggs

2 cups buttermilk

¼ cup honey

1 tablespoon melted butter

½ cup **hulled** sunflower seeds

maple syrup

butter

Directions:

Sift the dry ingredients into one mixing bowl. *Whisk* the eggs in the second bowl, add buttermilk, honey, melted butter; and whisk again. Pour the wet mixture into the dry mixture, and stir them together gently (the batter should remain somewhat lumpy). Add the sunflower seeds, and stir just to blend.

Dip a ¼-size measuring cup into the batter and use it to measure and pour batter onto the hot griddle. Make pancakes the size that you desire, but leave one inch between them for easier turning. When the edges of the pancake begin to dry, bubbles appear on the surface, and the bottom is lightly browned, it's time to flip the pancake over and cook the other side. Serve each stack of pancakes with a pat of cold butter and warm maple syrup.

Tips:

Strongly flavored heavy flours, like buckwheat and whole wheat, are usually mixed with white flour when baking or making pancakes. The same is true of cornmeal.

If you don't have buttermilk, put a tablespoon of lemon juice in a measuring cup and add milk to equal 1 cup.

It is not usually necessary to use cooking oil or vegetable spray when frying the pancakes on a griddle or in a nonstick skillet.

To know if your pancake griddle is hot enough to begin frying the pancakes, carefully throw a couple drops of water on the griddle's surface. If it quickly sizzles, pops, and evaporates, it's time to start cooking!

Midwest Food Facts

You'll find fields of sunflowers in Nebraska, South Dakota, and Kansas, but North Dakota is the nation's top producer. This state, whose motto is "strength from the soil," is also the number one producer of both honey and canola oil. Many other crops are grown here, including buckwheat and other types of wheat. In fact, people from North Dakota say that any time you eat spaghetti, you are most likely eating durum (one particular kind of wheat) from North Dakota.

Gingerbread Waffles

That great gingerbread flavor is not just for Christmas in the Midwest.

Cooking utensils you'll need:
3 mixing bowls
measuring cups
measuring spoons
wire whisk
waffle iron
oven-safe plate
aluminum foil
electric mixer

Ingredients:

1¼ cups flour
¼ cup sugar
¾ teaspoon baking soda
¼ teaspoon salt
1 teaspoon ginger
½ teaspoon cinnamon
¼ teaspoon ground cloves

1 egg
¼ cup sunflower or canola oil
¼ cup molasses
¼ cup hot water
1 cup whipping cream
1 tablespoon confectioners' sugar (powdered sugar)

Directions:

Lightly grease and preheat the waffle iron. Stir the flour, sugar, baking soda, salt, ginger, cinnamon, and cloves together in one mixing bowl. *Whisk* the egg, add the cooking oil, molasses, and hot water, and whisk again. Pour the wet mixture into the dry mixture. Beat well. Pour about 1/2 cup of the mixture onto the waffle iron, close the lid, and cook until done. (Cooking time can vary between different waffle irons.) Do not lift the lid until done, but be cautious to not overbake. Carefully lift the waffle from the iron.

Meanwhile, pour whipping cream into a mixing bowl, add confectioners' sugar, and beat on high until whipped. (Be careful not to overbeat or you'll end up with super sweet butter!) Serve each waffle with a *dollop* of whipped cream. This recipe makes three 7-inch waffles.

Tip:

Whipping cream beats more quickly if you chill the bowl and beaters in the refrigerator before beating.

You can also serve these waffles with applesauce or sour cream. Sweeten the sour cream with a little granulated sugar, if desired.

Unless a recipe instructs you to do otherwise, always use large eggs when baking.

Midwest Food Facts

Molasses was one of the major sweeteners used by farm families prior to the 1900s. In addition to sweetening baked goods, it is still often used in the Midwest to flavor baked beans. North Dakota is the number-one producer and Nebraska is the number-two producer of dry beans in the United States.

Grilled Swiss and Mushroom Burger

The Midwest is a major producer of beef, wheat, and cheese. Here the three combine perfectly in a mouth-watering burger.

Place the oven rack about 5 inches from the heat source, and preheat the broiler.

Ingredients:

1 pound lean ground beef
2 tablespoons Worcestershire sauce
2 tablespoons ketchup
½ teaspoon salt
dash pepper
1 tablespoon butter
1 cup sliced mushrooms
4 hamburger buns
¾ cup shredded Swiss cheese

Cooking utensils you'll need:
cheese shredder
mixing bowl
measuring cups
measuring spoons
skillet
2 broiler pans, cast-iron skillets, or other broiler-safe pans

Directions:

Shred cheese and set aside. Place the beef, Worcestershire sauce, ketchup, salt, and pepper in the mixing bowl, and stir them well. Shape into four equal-size patties (each about 1-inch thick), and put them in the broiling pan. Broil for about 8 minutes, turn the patties, and broil about another 8 minutes. (The meat should not be pink in the center when cooked.)

Meanwhile, after you turn the patties and begin cooking the second side, melt the butter in the skillet, and sauté mushrooms until cooked (about 3 or 4 minutes). Cut hamburger buns in half and place the bottoms in the second broiler pan.

Place a cooked burger on each bottom bun, and top with mushrooms and shredded cheese. Place top buns cut-side-up beside the bottom buns, and broil until cheese is melted and top buns are toasted. Place the bun tops cut-side-down on the burgers, and serve.

Tips:

It's easiest to cut fresh hamburger buns and other bread using a knife with a serrated edge.

If you like, add onions and lettuce to your burger.

Midwest Food Facts

Ohio produces more Swiss cheese than any other state in the union. Did you ever wonder why Swiss cheese has holes? They come from carbon dioxide that is trapped in the cheese curd when it's fermenting. Eat just one ounce of Swiss cheese, and you'll get 30 percent of the daily recommended allowance of calcium.

Deep-Dish Pizza

Ingredients:

1 cup lukewarm water
1 package active dry yeast
½ cup whole wheat flour
2 cups white flour
1 teaspoon salt
1 teaspoon sugar
olive oil
one 15½-ounce jar pizza sauce (any brand)
4 ounces pepperoni or sliced cooked sausage
8 ounces shredded mozzarella cheese
optional toppings (see "Tips")

Cooking utensils you'll need:
cheese shredder
mixing bowl
measuring cups
measuring spoons
deep-dish pizza pan or other pan with sides
wooden breadboard or other flat surface
clean dish towel

Directions:

Put lukewarm water in the mixing bowl, sprinkle the yeast over it, and stir to dissolve. Add the salt, sugar, 1 tablespoon of olive oil, the whole wheat flour, and 1 cup of the white flour. Mix well and add the remaining flour. When it becomes too stiff to stir with the spoon, use your hands, adding a little more flour as needed. (Do not to add too much flour, however, because the dough should remain somewhat moist.) Sprinkle a little flour on a wooden breadboard, and *knead* the dough for two or three minutes. Rub a little olive oil around the mixing bowl, place the dough back into it, rub a little oil on top of the dough, cover the bowl with a clean dish towel, and allow it to sit in a warm part of the kitchen for about an hour. (It is not necessary to wash the bowl before putting the dough back into it.)

Oil the pizza pan. Use your hands to spread the dough evenly in the oiled pan making sure it comes about halfway up the sides, cover with the towel again, and set aside. Shred the cheese, and prepare your choice of toppings. Preheat oven to 425°. Spread the pizza sauce evenly on the dough. Sprinkle each vegetable that you like across the pizza. Add pepperoni or cooked sausage and shredded cheese. Bake for 20 to 25 minutes. (When the pizza is done, the cheese will be melted and the crust lightly browned.)

Tips:

Boost the vitamin and mineral content of your pizza by personalizing it with favorite toppings. Some choices are: shredded carrots, chopped broccoli, chopped onions, chopped garlic, sliced ripe olives, sliced peppers, slivered spinach, and *slivered* basil leaves.

Some people like to bake the pizza crust for 5 minutes before adding the sauce and toppings.

Midwest Food History

Thanks for inventing the "deep-dish" pizza goes to Ric Riccardo and Ike Sewell of Pizzeria Uno. They came up with the idea in Chicago in 1943, and Americans have loved it ever since. So much so, in fact, that today one fourth of all the pizzas ordered in the United States are for this variety. Typically, the crust of deep-dish pizza is thicker, a little sweeter, and more bread- or cake-like than that of other pizza.

Sauerkraut Balls

Ingredients:

3 tablespoons butter
½ cup minced onion
1 garlic clove
¼ pound cooked ham, ground or **minced**
¼ pound corned beef, ground or minced
one 16-ounce can sauerkraut
1 tablespoon chopped parsley
¾ cup flour
½ cup beef broth
⅛ teaspoon nutmeg
dash of pepper
2 teaspoons mustard
dash of salt
2 eggs
2 tablespoons water
1½ cups dry bread crumbs
½ teaspoon paprika
canola oil

Cooking utensils you'll need:
3 mixing bowls
measuring cups
measuring spoons
garlic press
skillet
cookie sheet
long-handled slotted spoon
pan with deep sides for frying
candy thermometer

Directions:

Drain the sauerkraut, rinse with water, drain again, finely chop, and set it aside. Put butter in the skillet and place over medium heat. When butter is melted, add onion and use the garlic press to press garlic over the onion. (If you do not have a garlic press, mince the garlic.) Cook about 5 minutes and add meat. Cook until lightly browned, add sauerkraut, and continue cooking until moisture has evaporated. Stir in parsley and 1/4 cup of the flour. When meat is coated with flour, add beef broth. Cook until broth has thickened (usually about 2 minutes). Stir in nutmeg, pepper, and mustard, and pour into mixing bowl. Cover and chill in refrigerator.

Use your hands to form the cooled mixture into little balls (each about 1/2-inch in diameter). Put remaining flour and a dash of salt and pepper in a bowl. Whisk eggs, water, and a dash of salt and pepper in another bowl. Mix bread crumbs, paprika, and another dash of salt and pepper in the third bowl. Dredge the sauerkraut balls in flour, then egg, then bread crumbs, and place them on a cookie sheet.

Pour oil into the deep-sided pan to about 2-inches deep, insert candy thermometer, and heat to 365°. Use a long-handled slotted spoon to carefully place the balls in the oil, fry until golden brown (usually about 2 minutes) turning them with the spoon, and place on paper towels to drain off some of the oil. Serve hot.

Midwest Food History

Sauerkraut is one of the foods featured in Midwest communities with Germanic roots. Fermenting cabbage in salt was one method used to preserve the vegetable, and it helped add variety to winter meals.

Dairyland Cheddar Ring

Ingredients:

4 cups shredded or grated sharp cheddar cheese
¾ cup mayonnaise or salad dressing
½ cup **minced** onion
1 garlic clove
¼ teaspoon hot pepper sauce
1 cup raspberry preserves
small, fresh, mixed salad greens
crackers or fresh, crusty bread

Cooking utensils you'll need:
cheese shredder
mixing bowl
measuring cups
measuring spoons
garlic press
3 to 3½-cup ring mold (optional)
plastic wrap

Directions:

Grease the ring mold and set aside. Mix together the cheese, mayonnaise or salad dressing, and onion in the bowl. Using a garlic press, squeeze the garlic onto the mixture. (If you don't have a garlic press, mince the garlic.) Add the pepper sauce, and stir well. Put the mixture into the ring mold and press it well. Unmold the cheddar ring onto a serving plate by first placing an upside-down plate on top of the mold and then turning everything over. Cover the unmolded cheddar ring with plastic wrap and chill one hour. Just before serving, spread the cheddar ring with raspberry preserves and fill the hole in the center with salad greens. Place crackers or pieces of crusty bread around the ring just before serving.

Tips:

If you don't have a ring mold, you can use a bowl and make the cheese into a mound of that shape. Another alternative is to make the cheese into a log shape. If you use one of these methods, place the salad greens around the cheese, and serve the crackers or bread on the side.

Cheddar comes in mild, medium, and sharp varieties depending upon how long it has been aged. Use any type you prefer for this recipe.

Midwest Food Facts

Commonly referred to as "America's Dairyland," Wisconsin is a leader in milk, cheese, and butter production. In fact, the 1.2 million dairy cows in this state produce over thirteen percent of the United State's annual milk supply. Ninety-nine percent of the 17,800 dairy farms in Wisconsin are still family-owned and operated. In 1964, Wisconsin produced a giant cheddar cheese block for the New York State Fair. The cheese weighed 34,951 pounds!

  Did you ever wonder why some cheddar cheese is white and some is orange? Annatto, a food coloring that comes from a tropical tree, is added to make cheddar orange. White cheddar can be called Vermont Cheddar even when it doesn't come from Vermont.

Gelatin Pretzel Salad

*Salads and desserts prepared with JELL-O®, Cool Whip®, and similar conven-
ience foods became popular fare at Midwest picnics and church suppers.*

Preheat oven to 400 degrees Fahrenheit.

Ingredients:

2 cups crushed pretzels
3 tablespoons sugar
1 stick (¼-pound) butter, melted
one 8-ounce package cream cheese
2 cups whipped topping
2 small boxes instant strawberry gelatin
2 cups water
two 10-ounce packages frozen strawberries, sliced
one 20-ounce can crushed pineapple

Cooking utensils you'll need:
plastic bag
rolling pin
large mixing bowl
measuring cups
measuring spoons
saucepan
9-inch x 13-inch glass baking dish

Directions:

Place pretzels in the plastic bag, use the rolling pin to finely crush them, pour them into the mixing bowl. Mix in the sugar and melted butter. Press the mixture into the ungreased baking dish, bake for about 8 to 10 minutes, re-move from oven and let cool.

Cream the sugar and cream cheese together. Fold in the whipped topping, spread the mixture over the baked layer, and refrigerate.

Put the gelatin into the mixing bowl. Bring the water to a boil in the saucepan, pour it over the gelatin and stir to dissolve. Add the frozen straw-berries, and stir occasionally. When the strawberries are completely thawed, add the undrained pineapple, stir again, and refrigerate until the mixture just begins to thicken. Pour over the second layer, spread evenly, and refrigerate until the top layer is *set*. Serve this fruit salad cut into squares.

Midwest Food History

A carpenter and medicine manufacturer named Pearle B. Waite developed a convenient food in 1897. It was named JELL-O ® by his wife, May Davis Wait. Although it was not invented in the Midwest, its popularity quickly spread and by 1905 it was also being produced in Canada. In the early part of the twentieth century, immigrants received their first introduction to JELL-O while passing through Ellis Island. This may have helped to spread its popularity to the Midwest and elsewhere. By the 1930s and '40s, gelled salads were being made across America.

Hot German Potato Salad

Ingredients:

3 pounds small potatoes (new potatoes are best)
¼ teaspoon salt
8 slices bacon
1 onion, **diced**
2 stalks celery, diced
⅛ cup vinegar
¼ cup water
3 tablespoons sugar
1 tablespoon flour
1 tablespoon **minced** parsley
salt and pepper to taste

Cooking utensils you'll need:
stockpot
skillet
large mixing bowl
measuring cups
measuring spoons

Directions:

Put unpeeled whole potatoes into the stockpot and add enough water to cover them. Add the salt, bring to gentle boil, cover, and cook until potatoes are just done. When they are cool enough to handle, peel and slice or dice (whichever you prefer).

Fry the bacon in the skillet. When it is crisp, place the bacon on paper towels to drain off some of the fat. Put the onion and celery into the bacon fat that remains in the skillet. (There should be about 1/4 cup. If you have too much, discard some; if you have too little, add cooking oil.) Cook for 1 or 2 minutes.

Meanwhile, mix the vinegar, water, sugar, and flour together. Pour it into the skillet, and bring to a boil. Pour over the warm potatoes, add crumbled bacon and parsley, stir gently, add salt and pepper to taste, and serve hot.

Tip:

For a variation, add a teaspoon of dry or prepared mustard to the vinegar mixture.

Midwest Food History

Oscar Meyer first got into the meat business when he was only 14 years old. That's when the new immigrant became an apprentice at George Weber's Meat Market in Detroit. Eventually he moved to Chicago where he continued to work in the meat business. He was joined there by his brother, who had become a wurstmacher (someone who makes sausage) in Germany, and together they opened a store in a German neighborhood. Soon a third brother from Germany joined them, and their business expanded. When the United States created the Food Safety Inspection Service in 1906, the Meyers volunteered to have their products inspected, and in 1929 they began wrapping their Oscar Meyer® Wieners in a yellow paper band that included both the company name and a U.S. government inspection stamp. In 1924, Oscar Meyer received a patent to produce packaged sliced bacon.

Midwest Food History

Iowa's name comes from the Indian word *iowa*, meaning "beautiful land." It is known as the "Hawkeye State" in honor of Chief Black Hawk, a famous Sauk leader. Corn is Iowa's most important crop but it is also grown in many other parts of the Midwest. Indiana is the nation's largest producer of popcorn. You may be surprised at corn's many uses. As corn sweetener, it appears in marshmallows, soft drinks, candy, gum, mayonnaise, and countless other products. Corn also has many nonfood uses, for example as a fuel and in plastics, dyes, batteries, and crayons.

Iowa Corn Chowder

Ingredients:

¾ cup chopped onion
1 teaspoon butter (or margarine)
1 cup chopped celery
2 cups diced potatoes
2 cups chicken **stock** or vegetarian stock
1 bay leaf
2 cups chopped tomatoes
1½ cups corn kernels
1½ cups milk
½ cup chopped parsley
pinch of pepper

Cooking utensils you'll need:
large stockpot
measuring cups
measuring spoons

Directions:

In a large stockpot over medium-high heat, *sauté* onion in butter until soft but not browned. Add celery and potatoes and sauté for two minutes. Add stock and bay leaf to soup, and bring to a boil.

Lower heat to simmer and cook, covered, until potatoes are tender (about 20 minutes). Remove bay leaf and discard. Place 2 cups of the soup in a blender and *puree*. Return to pot. Add tomatoes, corn, and milk, and bring to a boil again. Lower heat and simmer for 5 minutes. Add parsley and pepper.

Tip:

If you don't want to make your own stock, you can use canned chicken broth for this recipe.

Swedish Meatballs

Ingredients:

3 tablespoons butter
¼ cup minced onion
¾ cup fresh bread crumbs
½ cup milk
½ pound lean ground beef
¼ pound ground pork
¼ pound ground veal
1 egg

½ teaspoon allspice
½ teaspoon nutmeg
¾ teaspoon salt
¼ teaspoon pepper
3 tablespoons flour
2 cups beef stock
½ cup heavy cream (whipping cream)
dash lemon juice

Directions:

Put 1 tablespoon butter in the small skillet, cook the onion in it until tender (about 5 minutes), cool. Mix the bread crumbs and milk in the small bowl, and set aside. Mix the three types of meat together in the large bowl, stir in the onion and the bread mixture, add spices, salt, and pepper, and mix well. Use your hands to make small meatballs (about 1-inch in diameter).

Put 2 teaspoons butter in the large skillet, place over medium heat, and cook the meatballs until browned all over, then place them on paper towels to drain off some of the fat. You won't be able to fit all the meatballs in the pan at once, so cook them in batches.

When all meatballs are cooked, stir the flour into the meat drippings remaining in the skillet. Cook and stir until lightly browned (usually about 3 minutes). *Whisk* in the beef stock until the flour lumps disappear. Place all of the meatballs back in the skillet, and cook for about 5 minutes (until the meatballs are hot and completely cooked through their centers). Pour in the cream, and bring to a gentle *simmer*. Stir in a dash of lemon juice, and serve.

Midwest Food History

Huge numbers of immigrants from Sweden began coming to the Midwest during the late 1860s. During this time, more than a million Swedes left their homeland for North America. They came looking for land, since in Sweden there were far more people than farms.

Wild Rice and Turkey Soup

Preheat oven to 350° Fahrenheit.

Ingredients:

8 cups water
1 teaspoon salt
1 cup wild rice
5 tablespoons butter
8 cups turkey stock (or chicken stock)
1 cup chopped onion
2 large carrots, chopped
2 celery stalks, finely chopped
1 teaspoon thyme
1 teaspoon rosemary
1 large potato, chopped
1 cup turkey pieces
salt and pepper to taste

Cooking utensils you'll need:
measuring cups
measuring spoons
saucepan
casserole dish with cover
stockpot

Directions:

Put the water, salt, and wild rice in the saucepan, and boil uncovered for 5 minutes. Drain off the water, and put the rice in the casserole dish. Mix in 1 tablespoon butter, then add 1 cup of the turkey or chicken stock. Bring the mixture to a boil, cover, and bake for about 35 minutes (until the rice is tender and the liquid is absorbed).

Put 4 tablespoons butter in the stockpot, place over medium heat, add the onion, and cook until tender and translucent (about 10 minutes), stirring occasionally. Stir in the carrots, celery, thyme, and rosemary. (If you are using dry rosemary, crush it a bit with your fingers before adding it to the pot.) Cook about 10 more minutes, stirring occasionally. Add the potato and remaining turkey or chicken stock, and *simmer* until the vegetables are tender (about 10 minutes). Stir in the wild rice and the meat, and cook 5 more minutes (until heated through). Add salt and pepper to taste before serving.

Tips:

Use fresh or dried herbs in this recipe.

For a variation, substitute chicken for the turkey. You can use canned meat broth or make your own by boiling turkey or chicken parts in water for a couple of hours.

Wild rice has a strong and unique flavor. You can use it in many recipes that call for rice, but you may want to mix it with other rice. It is also tasty when added to muffins, but be sure to cook the wild rice before adding it to muffin batter.

Midwest Food History

The Native Americans living in the area of Minnesota were the first to use wild rice, which isn't really rice at all. Wild rice comes from a particular type of grass that grows in shallow inland lakes. Indians used canoes to float among the grass and harvest the food in autumn. In the language of the Dakota Sioux, minisota means "sky-tinted water." Today, wild rice is the official "state grain" of Minnesota.

Minnesota also leads the nation in turkey production, bringing approximately 43½ million of the birds to market annually.

Midwest Food History

Northeastern Wisconsin is the only place in the world where Chicken Booyah is found. It is a favorite at festivals, church picnics, bazaars, and any other large gathering. Restaurants have their own special recipe. Booyah is sometimes called "Belgian penicillin," because it is believed to cure illnesses.

The word "booyah" may come from bouillon, a French word for broth. Another theory is that the word comes from the French word bouillir, meaning "to boil." When the first Belgian immigrants arrived in Wisconsin in 1853, they spoke their own version of French called "Walloon," and they may have written down their word for this soup just as they heard it, rather than with the correct French spelling.

Chicken Booyah

Ingredients:

1 chicken
2 large onions, cut in wedges
4 large carrots, cut in 1–inch pieces
½ bunch celery, cut in 1–inch chunks
3 large potatoes, cut in 1–inch chunks
1 to 2 teaspoons salt
½ to 1 teaspoon pepper
1 to 2 cups egg noodles

Cooking utensils you'll need:
large cooking pot
measuring spoons
measuring cups
paring knife

Directions:

Place the whole chicken in a large pot and pour in a gallon or more water to cover well. Add onion wedges and bring to a boil. Boil chicken 1 hour or until tender (the meat will fall easily from the bone). Lift the chicken from broth with tongs or two large forks and cool on a plate. Meanwhile, reduce the heat under the broth. Remove the bones from the chicken, cutting into large chunks where necessary. Return chicken to broth and add carrots, celery, and potatoes. Bring broth back to a boil, season to taste with salt and pepper, and cook 1 hour or longer. About 20 minutes before serving, add noodles and boil until noodles are tender. Serves 10 people.

Hash-Brown Casserole

Frozen potatoes make this dish convenient to prepare.

Preheat oven to 350° Fahrenheit.

Ingredients:

3 cups frozen hash-brown potatoes
¾ cup shredded cheese (cheddar or Monterey Jack)
1 cup cooked **diced** Canadian bacon (or cooked ham)
¼ cup sliced green onions
4 eggs
one 12-ounce can evaporated skim milk
⅛ teaspoon salt
⅛ teaspoon pepper

Cooking utensils you'll need:
cheese shredder
baking dish (1½- to 2-quart size)
mixing bowl
measuring cups
measuring spoons
wire whisk

Directions:

Grease baking dish and spread potatoes evenly across the bottom. Layer on the cheese, Canadian bacon or ham, and onion. *Whisk* the eggs in the mixing bowl. Add milk, salt, and pepper, and whisk again. Pour over the layered ingredients. Bake for 40 to 50 minutes (until the center is *set*).

Tip:

You can make this dish the day before and store it covered in the refrigerator until you're ready to bake it.

Midwest Food Tradition

Long-lasting produce like potatoes helped pioneer families make it through lean times. People in the Midwest have always seemed to crave hearty food as fuel against their weather extremes. In one six-month period during 1936, North Dakota recorded a high temperature of 121° Fahrenheit and a low temperature of -60° Fahrenheit! These are truly record-breaking extremes. In general, however, more moderately hot Midwestern summers help vegetables and grains to grow, and cold winters allow the soil to rest and become replenished for the next growing season.

Midwest Food History

Classic Wiener Schnitzel, which featured veal in the "old country" (Germany), has been given a new twist in the Midwest. Illinois, Indiana, and South Dakota are all noted for their thriving hog industries, making pork a logical choice for this classic dish. Many consider this variation even more flavorful than the original.

Wiener Schnitzel—Midwestern Style

Ingredients:

4 boneless pork cutlets or chops (about ½-inch thick)
¾ cup flour
1 teaspoon salt
¼ teaspoon pepper
2 eggs
2 tablespoons water
2 cups fine, dry bread crumbs
2 tablespoons butter
2 tablespoons cooking oil

Cooking utensils you'll need:
waxed paper
wooden mallet
measuring cups
measuring spoons
plate or plastic bag
wire whisk
2 mixing bowls
skillet

Directions:

The meat should be about ¼-inch thick when you cook it. To achieve this and to tenderize it, put each piece of meat between two sheets of waxed paper and pound it with the mallet.

Mix together the flour, salt, and pepper on the plate or in a bag. *Whisk* the eggs and water in a bowl. Put the bread crumbs in a separate bowl.

Dredge meat in flour mixture, one piece at a time. Then dip it in the egg mixture. Third, dredge it in bread crumbs. Put butter and oil in skillet over medium/high heat, and fry the coated meat until golden brown (about 2 to 4 minutes per side).

Tips:

If necessary, use a fork to press the bread crumbs onto the meat.

If you like sage, add some to the bread crumbs.

Midwest Food Facts

Indiana is America's second largest producer of tomatoes for processing. Interestingly, in some ways processed tomatoes are healthier for you than fresh ones. That's because processed tomatoes are loaded with lycopene, an important antioxidant. Antioxidants help to counteract free radicals, the "bad guys" that contribute to many illnesses including heart disease and cancer.

Indiana Meatloaf

Preheat oven to 350° Fahrenheit.

Ingredients:

2¾ pounds lean ground beef
1¼ teaspoons salt
¼ teaspoon nutmeg
1 tablespoon parsley
3 garlic cloves
1 cup finely chopped onions
½ cup finely chopped celery

2 eggs
⅓ cup ketchup
¾ cup fresh bread crumbs
4 slices bacon (optional)
one 28-ounce can plum tomatoes
1 tablespoon extra virgin olive oil
¼ teaspoon red pepper flakes

Cooking utensils you'll need:
large mixing bowl
measuring cups
measuring spoons
garlic press
9-inch x 13-inch glass baking dish
9-inch-square second baking dish

Directions:

Put the meat into the large mixing bowl, and stir in 1 teaspoon of the salt. Add nutmeg and parsley, and stir again. Using the garlic press, squeeze 2 garlic cloves onto the meat. (If you don't have a garlic press, *mince* the garlic.) Stir well, and add the onion, celery, eggs, and ketchup. Mix again, and add the bread crumbs. Stir well, and mound into an oval in the center of the large baking dish. Drape the bacon slices over the meatloaf, and bake a total of about 70 minutes.

Meanwhile, pour the undrained tomatoes into the smaller baking dish. Slice each tomato in half, and add the extra virgin olive oil, remaining salt, and pepper flakes. Use the garlic press to press the remaining garlic over the mixture, and stir. When the meatloaf has baked for about 30 minutes, place the pan of tomatoes in the oven next to the meatloaf, and bake for about 40 minutes. Use a turkey baster to drain off fat from around the meatloaf, and spoon the tomatoes and sauce around the meatloaf before serving.

Tip:

You can use ground turkey or a mixture of ground beef, veal, and pork in place of the beef in this recipe.

Country Pot Roast

Preheat oven to 325° Fahrenheit.

Ingredients:

4- to 5-pound beef bottom round
or rump roast
¾ teaspoon salt
¼ teaspoon pepper
2 tablespoons sunflower or canola oil
3 cups chopped onion
4 garlic cloves
2 large carrots
2 ribs celery
4 parsnips

2 bay leaves
1 teaspoon thyme
one 14-½ ounce can whole tomatoes
two 14-ounce cans beef broth
1 tablespoon cornstarch
½ cup cold water
fresh parsley
hot cooked egg noodles

Cooking utensils you'll need:
Dutch oven
measuring cups
measuring spoons
garlic press
oven-safe platter
aluminum foil
stock pot
vegetable strainer
large bowl

Directions:

Cut the carrots, celery, and parsnips into pieces that are about 2-inches long. Drain and chop the tomatoes (see "Tips"). Wash the roast, and pat it dry with paper towels. Put about 1½ tablespoons of the oil into the Dutch oven, and place over medium heat. Sprinkle all sides of the roast with 1/4 teaspoon salt and pepper. Place the meat in the pan, brown all sides, and remove from pan.

Put onions in the pan, and cook until soft. Using the garlic press, press garlic into the pan. (If you don't have a garlic press, finely *mince* the garlic.) Add the remaining vegetables and thyme, and cook for about 5 minutes. Stir in the tomatoes and ½ teaspoon salt, and cook for another 5 minutes. Add beef broth and bay leaves, bring to boil, place the roast on top, cover, and bake for 1 hour. Remove from oven, turn the roast over, replace cover, and bake another 1½ to 2 hours. Turn the oven off, remove roast from pan, place on oven-safe platter, cover with aluminum foil, and return to warm oven.

Meanwhile, cook egg noodles in the stockpot according to package directions.

Meanwhile, place the vegetable strainer on the large bowl, and strain the vegetables to separate them from the broth. Scrape any small vegetable pieces that stick to the strainer back into the broth. Pour the broth back into the Dutch oven. Mix the cornstarch into the cold water, pour into the broth, stir to dissolve any lumps, and simmer gently for about 2 minutes stirring occasionally.

Slice the meat and arrange it on a serving plate. Place the vegetables around it. Spoon broth over the meat, and garnish the plate with parsley. Place the egg noodles in a serving bowl, and mix in 1 teaspoon oil to prevent the noodles from sticking together.

Tips:

Freeze the juice from the canned tomatoes and add it to soup.

To add extra vitamins and color contrast to the noodles, cook 1 cup of frozen peas, and mix them with the noodles just before serving.

Midwest Food Facts

Root vegetables, like the carrots and parsnips in this recipe, lasted a long time in root cellars. They were among the staple foods that helped early Midwest farm families make it through harsh winters.

Spaetzle

Ingredients:

3 eggs
1 cup milk
¼ teaspoon salt
2 cups flour
1 tablespoon butter
salt and pepper to taste

Directions:

Put a large amount of water in the stockpot, add a little salt, and bring to a gentle boil. Put the flour in a mixing bowl, and form a "hole" in the center. Put the eggs in the second mixing bowl, and *whisk*, add milk and salt, and whisk again. Pour the egg mixture into the center of the flour, and stir until the batter is smooth. Put a big spoonful of batter onto a plate, and use a butter knife to move some of it to the plate's edge. Carefully hold the plate above the boiling water, and use the knife to cut thin pieces of dough along the plate's edge, allowing them to drop into the water. The pieces should be about an inch long. The squiggly dumplings rise to the surface when they are cooked (usually in about 1 minute). Boil the dumplings in batches, and use the slotted spoon to remove them as they are cooked.

Put the butter in a skillet and place over medium/high heat. Add some of the boiled spaetzle, and fry (stirring occasionally) until they are lightly browned (usually about 2 minutes). Repeat with the remaining spaetzle. Add salt and pepper to taste, and serve hot.

Tip:

Here's another easy way to form the dumplings. Use a cake-decorating bag or, for even easier clean-up, use a heavy-duty disposable plastic bag with the corner cut off. Put the batter in the bag and squeeze, dropping tiny amounts of dough into the boiling water.

Midwest Food History

Parts of the Midwest landscape are still dotted with the homes of German immigrants. Spaetzle (pronounced SHPET-sluh) is a specialty of southwestern Germany (called Swabia) and comes from the German word for sparrow. Perhaps the sight of these small dumplings floating in water reminded German cooks of a flock of little birds. This is a great side dish for pot roast, but it is also delicious with roast chicken.

Creamed Whitefish

Preheat oven to 400° Fahrenheit.

Ingredients:

8 small whitefish fillets
½ cup **minced** celery
1 cup heavy cream (whipping cream)
2 tablespoons butter
salt and pepper

Directions:

Wash the fish and pat it dry with paper towels. Grease the baking pan with butter and place the fish in it. Put cream in the saucepan and bring it to a boil over medium heat (stir occasionally, being careful not to allow the cream to burn). Immediately remove it from the heat, add celery and just one or two shakes of salt and pepper, and pour it over the fish. Bake for about 8 minutes (until the fish flakes easily when poked with a fork).

Tip:

Substitute other types of fish for the whitefish in this recipe.

Cooking utensils you'll need:
measuring cups
measuring spoons
saucepot
baking dish

Midwest Food Tradition

The Upper Midwest, consisting of Michigan, Wisconsin, and Minnesota, is home to more than 37,000 inland lakes. In addition to that, each of these states has shorelines on the Great Lakes. Minnesota borders Lake Superior, Wisconsin borders Lake Superior and Lake Michigan, and Michigan has borders on four of the Great Lakes—Lake Superior, Lake Michigan, Lake Erie, and Lake Huron. No matter where you are in any of these states, you are always close to a lake where you can fish.

Deep-water fish are a food tradition along the Great Lakes in the Upper Midwest. This vacation land is filled with restaurants offering all manner of fish specialties, including "fish boils" where fish are often boiled with potatoes and other ingredients in pots that are so big they have to be placed over outdoor fires.

Chunky Cherry Cobbler Ice Cream

Preheat oven to 350° Fahrenheit.

Ingredients:

1 cup rolled oats (quick cooking or old-fashioned)
½ cup flour
½ cup brown sugar, firmly packed
½ teaspoon cinnamon
⅓ cup melted butter
1 small box vanilla pudding mix (cook-and-serve type)
2 cups sugar
***dash** salt*
4 cups light cream (half-and-half)
6 eggs
one 21-ounce can cherry pie filling
1 teaspoon vanilla
2 cups whole milk

Cooking utensil you'll need:
mixing bowl
measuring cups
measuring spoons
jelly roll pan
large saucepan
wire whisk
4- to 5-quart ice cream freezer

Directions:

Put the rolled oats, flour, brown sugar, and cinnamon in the mixing bowl. Stir, add the melted butter, and stir again. Spread the mixture on the jelly roll pan, bake for 9 or 10 minutes, stir, return to oven, and bake until lightly browned (about 9 more minutes). Remove the cobbler crunch from the oven, and allow it to cool while you make the ice cream.

Put the pudding mix, sugar, and salt in the saucepan. Stir, add milk, and stir again. Place over medium heat, and cook until bubbly and thickened, stirring constantly. Mix in the light cream, and continue cooking and stirring for another 2 minutes.

Whisk the eggs in the mixing bowl. Add about 1/4 cup of the hot mixture to the eggs, whisking constantly to prevent the eggs from cooking. Add about 2 more cups of the hot mixture to the eggs in the same manner. Pour the egg mixture into the remaining hot mixture in the saucepan, stirring constantly. Cook the mixture for 2 more minutes, stirring constantly, and then remove it from the heat.

Stir the cherry pie filling and vanilla into the hot mixture, and allow it to cool. Pour the cooled mixture into an ice cream freezer, add milk, freeze according to manufacturer's directions. Remove the dasher, stir in the cobbler crunch, ripen the ice cream, and enjoy.

Midwest Food History

The name Michigan comes from the Algonquin Indian word michigama, which means "great lake." Growing conditions for tart cherries are perfect along the Lake Michigan coast, helping to make Michigan the number-one producer of tart cherries in the nation. Michigan is also the top producer of cucumbers grown for pickles as well as being among the top three states for apples, celery, carrots, and asparagus.

Meanwhile, Two Rivers, Wisconsin is credited as being the birthplace of the ice cream sundae in 1881. According to the legend, it happened in an ice cream parlor when a customer asked that some of the chocolate syrup reserved for making ice cream sodas be placed on his dish of ice cream. The treat quickly became popular, and soon nuts and other toppings were also being offered. An ice cream parlor in another town also began offering the dish, but only on Sunday—hence the origin of the name.

Ohio "Buckeye" Candy

Ingredients:

2 sticks (½ pound) butter
4½ cups confectioners' sugar (powdered sugar)
one 16-ounce jar crunchy peanut butter
one 12-ounce bag chocolate chips
1 square inch chunk paraffin wax

Directions:

Put the paraffin and chocolate chips in the saucepan, place over low heat, and cook until melted, stirring occasionally.

Meanwhile, mix the butter and peanut butter together in the mixing bowl. *Cream* in the sugar. Use your hands to make the mixture into small balls (about 1 inch in diameter) and place them on the cookie sheet. Dip one half of each ball in the melted chocolate and place it (chocolate side up) on the cookie sheet.

Tip:

These candies can be made ahead of time and frozen until use.

Midwest Food Tradition

The official state tree of Ohio is the buckeye. Perhaps this candy acquired its name because the round chocolate confections reminded cooks of the buckeye's unhusked fruit.

Further Reading

Fertig, Judith M. *Prairie Home Cooking*. Boston, Mass.: Harvard Common Press, 1999.

Gunderson, Mary. *The Food Journal of Lewis & Clark: Recipes for an Expedition*. Yankton, S.D.: History Cooks, 2003.

Loomis, Susan Herrmann. *Farm House Cookbook*. New York: Workman Publishing, 1991.

Madison, Deborah. *Local Flavors: Cooking and Eating From America's Farmers' Markets*. New York: Broadway Books, 2002.

Stern, Jane. *The Harry Caray's Restaurant Cookbook: The Official Home Plate of the Chicago Cubs*. Nashville, Tenn.: Rutledge Hill Press, 2003.

Werlin, Laura, *The New American Cheese: Profiles of America's Great Cheesemakers and Recipes for Cooking with Cheese*. New York: Stewart, Tabori & Chang, 2000.

For More Information

Facts about Cheese
www.nederland.k12.tx.us/links/cheese.htm

Kitchen Safety
www.premiersystems.com/recipes/kitchen-safety/cooking-safety.html

Midwest Meat Recipes
www.cloverdalefoods.com/listrecipe.php?so=flavor&set=Midwest

Midwest Organic Alliance (Definition of Organic Foods Plus Recipes)
www.organic.org/3/index.html

Midwest Recipes
www.recipezaar.com/r/291

State Agricultural Profiles
www.agclassroom.org

Upper Midwest History
memory.loc.gov/ammem/umhtml/umessay0.html

Publisher's note:
The Web sites listed on this page were active at the time of publication. The
publisher is not responsible for Web sites that have changed their addresses or
discontinued operation since the date of publication. The publisher will review
and update the Web sites upon each reprint.

Index

Author:

In addition to writing, Joyce Libal has worked as an editor for a half dozen magazines, including a brief stint as recipe editor at *Vegetarian Gourmet*. Most of her experience as a cook, however, has been gained as the mother of three children and occasional surrogate mother to several children from different countries and cultures. She is an avid gardener and especially enjoys cooking with fresh herbs and vegetables and with the abundant fresh fruit that her husband grows in the family orchard.

Recipe Tester / Food Preparer:

Bonni Phelps owns How Sweet It Is Café in Vestal, New York. Her love of cooking and feeding large crowds comes from her grandmothers on both sides whom also took great pleasure in large family gatherings.

Consultant:

The Culinary Institute of America is considered the world's premier culinary college. It is a private, not-for-profit learning institution, dedicated to providing the world's best culinary education. Its campuses in New York and California provide learning environments that focus on excellence, leadership, professionalism, ethics, and respect for diversity. The institute embodies a passion for food with first-class cooking expertise.

Recipe Contributor:

Patricia Therrien has worked for several years with Harding House Publishing Service as a researcher and recipe consultant—but she has been experimenting with food and recipes for the past thirty years. Her expertise has enriched the lives of friends and family. Patty lives in western New York State with her family and numerous animals, including several horses, cats, and dogs.

Picture Credits